Praise for Isn't It Rich?

"A hilarious, sparkling, and rowdy *Looseleaves Of Grass!* A joyous yawp, with dry martinis, frozen swans, and jeroboams of style. Huzzah that the best poetry can be fun again!"
~ Sandra Tsing Loh, Performer and Author,
The Madwoman In The Volvo

"Victoria Looseleaf's name would suggest inspired scribblings in a spiral notebook. Inspired, yes, but also beautifully crafted. Leaving prose behind and working in a poetic form has miraculously clarified her insights, deepened her humor and brought her even closer to her readers. This is a wonderful book, always surprising and great fun to read."
~ Charles Busch, Actor, Tony Award Nominated Playwright and Drag Legend

"I love it! Victoria's poetry is... richly raw, wild and witty, wonderfully funny and sad, sensual and serious, brilliant and endearing!"
~ Daniel Ezralow, Award-Winning Director, Choreographer and Performer

"Victoria Looseleaf's poems are beautiful autobiographical short stories full of wit and grace. *Isn't It Rich?* Indeed it is."
~ Larry Karaszewski, Award-Winning Filmmaker

"Bravo Victoria! This collection of passionate poems, transports, engages and provokes thought. Many read-

Praise for Isn't It Rich?

ers will quickly cast their favorites to be reread again and again.
    ~ Desmond Richardson, Tony Award Nominee and Performer

"Read Looseleaf's poetry and you will get a glimpse of a free spirit with a lust for life: plenty of sex, plenty of self-loathing and plenty of entertainment. Looseleaf has never met a surfer she didn't want to fuck. This is poetry that lets you forget you're reading poetry, and that's a good thing."
    ~ Tulsa Kinney, Editor of *Artillery*

"Victoria Looseleaf, respected dance critic, has had quite a life. In a small book of poems, she reveals she has apparently been everywhere, loved wildly and well, yet had time to reflect philosophically and with humor. Pacific coast surfers, buy this book. You owe her.'
    ~ Steve Paxton, Dancer and Choreographer

"Playful and supple with an exotic sexy roasted nut and dark fruit character and perfectly balanced with a refreshing level of racy acidity. Pair with a box of truffles or read by itself, if you dare!"
    ~ John Fleck, Actor and Performance Artist

"Finally a poet that captures with brutal honesty, the undeniable draw that surfers and surfing have on our culture. Her poems are like orgasms that make you want to laugh and cry at the same time."
    ~ John Philbin, Professional Surfer, Producer and Actor

Praise for Isn't It Rich?

"Uncannily colorful, erotic, whimsical, musical, and funny, Victoria's poetry makes the blood course more urgently through my veins and paints the kind of vivid world in which I feel alive. She makes me want to play my violin and make a beautiful cacophony."
    ~ Lili Haydn, Violinist, Vocalist and Composer

"These charming, clever and compelling recollections of a fully lived and well-traveled life breathe new life into autobiographical verse and commit the unforgivable poetic sin of being accessible and entertaining."
    ~ John Tottenham, Poet and Author
        The Inertia Variations and *Antiepithalamia*

"An emotional travelogue to exotic landscapes, mindscapes and bodyscapes. Looseleaf tells her life story in poetry the way a stone skips over water. High point to high point, then sinking in to the bottom of the pond, exploring the dark depths. Funny, heartfelt, smart and sexy."
    ~ Beth Lapides, Comedian and *UnCabaret* Creatrix

"*Isn't It Rich? A Novella in Verse* was like hitchhiking through time and space in a convertible without the regulatory encroachment of a seat belt. Something liberating bursts forth in Looseleaf's verse. While careening around her curves of thought and sweeping through her autobiographical landscapes, I laughed out loud, felt the pangs of loss, smiled in familiar awareness, and

Praise for Isn't It Rich?

did more than a few double takes. A fantastic assemblage of a life stretched out over the clang and rattle of modern change."
 ~ Kristy Edmunds, Artistic and Executive Director, Center for the Art of Performance, UCLA

"Ms. Looseleaf has never failed to impress with her sharp wit and this collection doesn't disappoint. Some passages make you laugh so hard, and then make you worry that you're a terrible person for laughing. And then you immediately realize, yes, that is the point! This is iron-fist-in-velvet-glove stuff of the highest order."
 ~ Benny Rietveld, Musical Director, *Santana*

"*Isn't It Rich?* is like drinking water in the greenery of a mountain spring. It is clear, refreshing and vibrant. It's a generation's story presented as a kaleidoscopic aqua-ballet; it's imagery permutating in all directions from its center. Ms. Looseleaf's voice is natural. Her stories told with humor and charm, all shot through with song. Memoir and music meet in this volume. Her writing seems effortless but Ms. Looseleaf has a great deal of craft. Even its table of contents is structured as a poem. A remarkable achievement."
 ~ Darius James, Author *Negrophobia* and Performance Artist

"Victoria Looseleaf is a tall, thin, female Bukowski with good skin who is bent on bedding all in her cultural path. *Isn't It Rich?* is her confession."
 ~ Mary Woronov, Actress, Artist and Writer

Isn't It Rich?

A Novella In Verse

Victoria Looseleaf

GORDY GRUNDY
PUBLISHERS

This is a work of fiction. Names, characters, places, and incidents are the products of the author's imagination or are used fictiously. Any resemblance to actual events, locales or persons, living or dead, is entirely coincidental.

ISN'T IT RICH?

Copyright © 2015 Victoria Looseleaf

2015 Gordy Grundy Press Trade Paperback Edition

All Rights Reserved.

Published in the United States of America

Cover Art by Katrien De Blauwer

Photography by Mark Hanauer
Hair & Make-Up: Gigi Gullihur   Stylist Claudia Rossini

Concept, Edit and Book Design by Gordy Grundy

ISBN-13: 978-0692572092
ISBN-10: 0692572090
Library of Congress Control Number: 2015918644

www.Victoria Looseleaf.com

GORDY GRUNDY
PUBLISHERS
www.GordyGrundy.com

For my father, a rock who has always been there for me, to the memories of my brother Ritchie, my amazing mother Bernice, my beautiful nephew Dylan and my Renaissance man, Taylor Negron, forever in my heart. Inspirations, all.

ACKNOWLEDGMENTS

I am blessed to be surrounded by so many huge-hearted people to whom I owe an eternal debt of gratitude. My profound thanks go to Kate Johnson, Larry ("Daddy G") Gilbert, Russ Butler, John Fleck, Lita Albuquerque, Carey Peck, Jasmine Albuquerque Croissant, Mark Schwartz, Rudy Perez, Joanna Cottrell, Lili Haydn, Sussan Deyhim, Kenneth Hughes, Melissa Carrey, Neal Taylor, Mike M. Mollett, Dee Balson Mollett, Mark Hanauer, Mary Woronov, Gigi Gullihur, Ryan Jimenez, Larry Weinstein, Penelope Ford, James Goldman, Bruno Duluc-Daniel, Claudia Rossini, Tricia Noble, Maryellen McGrath, Maggie Rowe, Charlotte Spiegelman, Peggy Stark, Dr. Irwin Miller, Dr. Herb Glicksman and Joyce (La Chanteuse Dangereuse) Aimee, as well as to my brothers Brian and Gary, my sister-in-abstentia, Kathy Lee W.M.S.J., and my stepmother Esther.

In addition, I offer *besos* and *merci beaucoup* to Jacques Heim and all of those insanely beautiful dance gods and goddesses who continually lift me up with their art. And, finally, my deepest appreciation goes to my unflappable and talented editor, Gordy Grundy, and San Francisco's King of Poetry, Philip Hackett, whose unerring way with words has been a guiding light through the years.

Isn't It Rich?
Victoria Looseleaf

I.

QUEEN OF THE SURF 19
WHEELS OF LOVE 21
ENTERING THE ALPHABET 25
ZEN WAS NEVER LIKE THIS BEFORE 27

II.

ON TONGUES 31
RADICAL GODDESS 33
WATCHING THE NEEDLE 35
AN ICHTHYOLOGICAL TALE 37
ON BEDS AND THEIR OCCUPANTS 41

III.

SAY HELLO TO A BEAUTIFUL LADY 45
SMILE 47
BACK TO PARADISE 49
ANOTHER YANKEE IN ARS LONGA 53

IV.

SUNDAY IN THE POOL WITH FRED 59
MOTHER LOVE 63
THE LIFE OF A SHRIMP 65
LIFESTYLES OF THE POOR AND UNKNOWN 67

V.

THE GENETICS OF DINING 73
A SWEET TOOTH FILLS THE AIR 75
AS LONG TWILIGHT CALLS 77

VI.

A FAR CRY FROM GITCHE GUMEE 81
THIS POEM LAUGHS 85
MA 87

VII.

ORDER IN THE AIR 93
THE CLOT THICKENS 95
BEAN CAKES AND YOU 97

VIII.

SCREWTOPIA 101
SOMETHING FISHY 103

IX.

NEO-HAIKUS AND THINGS 109
NOT THE RITZ 111
THE DANCE CRITIC 113
THIS VERY MOMENT 117

Vissi d'arte, vissi d'amore

It has been my experience, reflecting on life, that when you hold a mirror up to nature, make sure it's attached to a wall.

So, dear ones, keep your hands free at all times.

~ Victoria Looseleaf

Isn't It Rich?

Isn't It Rich?

I.

QUEEN OF THE SURF

Practicing for the long altar walk,

I start in Cleveland,
head west through Tucson
and plunge into the Pacific,
with a series of surfers
who don't speak marriage,
they speak on wavelengths
of *"Fuck me now, baby,
and wax my board."*

We talk in sign language,
my sign is
Bienvenidos, Open All Night.

They stop by for an evening,
hang ten and stay a month.
They're a curious breed these surfers
they have highly developed back muscles
and very evolved knees.

I fall to mine and we're all happy
with this regimen.

My psychiatrist tells me to find
an appropriate man – someone about 40.
Next week I pick up two surfers, ages 19
and 20.

"That makes 39," I say, *"will that do?"*

I never lived on the ocean before and
find the surf ilk a fascinating one.
I buy binoculars and bring home
my catch of the day nightly.

I look for a long white wet suit
with a veil and high-heeled flippers.
Ohio could be the moon now
as I prepare to ride the next wave,

foaming with desire I
catch the crest
feel the wind in my hair
the sun on my cheeks
a pounding in my heart.
I'm in the tube
taking it all the way
when a smile beams forth
and I shout with the sea:

I may have gone out a spinster, world,

a lonely girl from the shores of Lake Erie,

but you better believe that I'm now sailing in,

irrefutably

indomitably

and in perfect form,

The Queen of the Surf.

WHEELS OF LOVE

I am the only passenger wheeled off the
plane into the Cartagena airport.
It is the middle of a December hot night
in South America and cocaine is just a
friendly little drug
used by Freud
a handful of Incas
and me.

We get a cabbie who cruises us the long
way around the walled city.
When the sun rises
I am desperate for Chinese food
and a pain pill.

My wheels are starting to rust so I go for
huaraches and a string bikini by the pool,
a high-rise waterway shaped like
a mushroom.

We sauté for a while and knock back a few
agua calientes,
fire waters.

"*Holy Christ,*" I say,
slipping from
New York consciousness
my mind stuck in housewares at Bloomingdale's
and the Cuisinart's about to blow.

I wake up in suite 502 and a
huge brown maid stands over me

shaking her Alka Seltzer and singing *Feliz Navidad*.
I drink the stuff and prepare to be kissed.

Worse things have happened.

Shere and I sport matching holly wreathes
and wind up at the Blue Parrot nightclub,
Mai Tais in hand, we wait for the show
paseoing around the room
getting jabbed by paper umbrellas. The
clientele begins to look suspect:

The men are women and the women are all in Rio.
We soon discover
we are the show and
Jesus is just around the corner with Carl Sagan.

How does a nice Jewish girl like me
always wind up in the crossfire
between bacon and eggs?

Our driver high-tails us over to the casino
where 21 is played in Spanish
and the New Year's bell begins to toll.

"*Veintiuno,*" I cry
scooping up the chips
licking my salty lips and
laying it all on the line.

I close my eyes and see the
end of the rainbow.

The wheelchair is oiled and ready to go
but
I
walk
up
the
ramp
myself.

ENTERING THE ALPHABET

        Entering the alphabet I pause at

the f and think

of you

fucking

you

fuck is on the brain a lot

getting horny

wanting a man around

only to meet with

more screwballs

lame duck lawyers

fanatics

and crap at the checkout counter

        I could use a pedicure

but haven't gotten to the $p's$ yet.

ZEN WAS NEVER LIKE THIS BEFORE

I run off to Mexico when I am nineteen and
marry Rick
in a black lace cocktail dress
eating blue corn tortillas.

He is walking away from the draft,
a selective service
wind blows cold gusts of air
up my thighs
and puts him away for six years.

The desert jail
makes us all thirsty
and I wonder if my wig is on straight
in the courtroom
when the judge looks at me
with gavel eyes
and my beige linen dress wrinkles
from the heat of it all.

They call me a character witness
but who, really, is the character,
I think, so young
and so gullible
I can't even cook for myself.

I bring Rick Hershey Bars and kisses,
apples and psilocybin mushrooms.
It is Halloween and
the trick is to slip into his cell
like a good little ghost.
I'm friendly and white
the guards like that
and so does Rick.

That weekend we go to
Kathmandu, Fiji and Machu Picchu.
The mountain's high but we've got
good boots
not those fur-lined mules my
mother wears, smoking three packs of Kools and
knitting angora pullovers for
rich women cruising the Caribbean.

Which river do you take to Safford, Arizona,
the pizza-colored monolith of dark men who
dig ditches and pound out license plates?

I spend the night at a Quality Inn,
killing a roach and
sleeping with the pole lamp
burning forty watts.

"How many miles to the border?" I ask.

"Which one, missy?"

"Any one, I s'pose, Mexico, Nevada, California."

I don't see that it matters much anymore,
walking the edge
like I do.

I get in my van and drive south.
The sun is pink when I see Rick's face in my
mind's-eye mirror.

Zen was never like this before.

II.

ON TONGUES

        Tongues can be very sexy
when they're not being vicious
mine is quick on both counts and I'm looking
for a suitable match
similarly proportioned

        A well-heeled tongue
a hearty tongue
a sweet tongue
a tongue on rye with plenty of mustard
might be okay, too

        Do I advertise
do I synthesize
do I fantasize?

All of the above I surmise,
providing the tongue is not tied to
any apron strings
though I hear that forked tongues are good in the kitchen

        An overworked tongue can be very trying
but a twisted one works wonders
on my lower anatomy

        I'm also told that tungsten burns
hottest at night
when the moon is low
so I'm lying on my bed early tonight
keeping the moon in full view

and sticking to tongue teasers
like you, baby

>*Why don't you roll over and kiss me,
>then, huh!*

RADICAL GODDESS

i was a radical goddess
they loved me on campus
i wore khaki camouflaged raincoats
in the midday sun
no make-up
no bra
no problems

where was i going?
am i there now?

how will i recognize
that life again
unless this is it
living hard in a low-rise apartment
in a strange city overrun with
cars and herbaceous brains
robots and tuesday
oppressions

i climb the walls like bougainvillea,
burning pink and orange, i call
attention to myself
look towards the sky
eternally cloudless
tell myself lots of big stories
and cry myself to sleep

eat some greens
sweat it out at the gym
look at

all the different bodies
in one kind of mind

why do i know these people
when they'll never know me?

WATCHING THE NEEDLE

run run run da doo run
running
around with nowhere to go
filling the tank then
watching the needle make its descent towards *E*
only to rise again triumphant
an occasional *F*

her life's on *E* most of the time too
da doo run run run da
doing
the banal to make ends meet
so she can have some beginnings now and then

a little love wouldn't hurt either

i've got tuesdays free,
every other friday
and all night long for the rest of my life

she boppa woppa loola she
wants to fill up her dance card
is this such a tragedy?
make out good, have a kid
a house with a tree, not necessarily palm
someone to cry on when she hurts
someone to cook for
just
someone

she boppa woppa she
do run run run

she do run
in circles these days

and before she knows it
she's running out of steam
runs into the ground
lies down
takes a last breath
calls it quits
and joins an over-the-hill rock and roll band

da doo run run run
da doo run run

AN ICHTHYOLOGICAL TALE

what about the herring

sitting in a bowl of white cream
reminding me of my own hot sex
telling me
it's time to be a mother already
before the clock goes berserk

who's going to fertilize me
give me a flower
a crossbreed i might call azalea
fork out the fish
stir it around
smell it
and love it because it is
good

walk into the fast living room
thru another door where I might find
some love or at least
a little blast in the night
drink the water
balance a chunk of cheese
on my tongue and tell a crowd of new old faces

*i'm from the midwest
via tokyo
amsterdam and miami beach*

it was a hand-to-houseboat life on the prinsengracht

i say
feeling grimy on the canals
but free just the same
free to
study van gogh's *starry night*
and then smoke hashish on the street with a touring housewife
from des moines

there was no time for responsibility and
one month bled into the next like madras

jazz gets louder now so i listen
to another voice drone on instead
my memories are enough for me but
why push them on a stranger

this love will take time
i decide,
if it even takes at all

i sink into the chintz and think about mr. tee
in tokyo

i had fallen in love with his madly
oscillating blue eyes but realized
our situation would require a lot of money
and a chauffeur

i'll wait
i tell him
leaving that strange city
of 12 million others
where serenity is a rock garden
covered with freshly fallen snow

i continue to stare ahead at the fish platter and
wonder just what it is

i am waiting for.

ON BEDS AND THEIR OCCUPANTS

This is the last payment on my

bed. It's still empty, too,

except for me,

an arrangement

I wouldn't have thought

would go on this long,

but some things, like beds and their occupants,

are never predictable.

Isn't It Rich?

III.

SAY HELLO TO A BEAUTIFUL LADY

Ready to land in New York again July 4th
with the Statue of Liberty showing me
her hot torch.
I was once one of the tired she
talked about before I went into a
coma
trying to forget my life on the
concrete island.

I used to walk those streets searching for
Bob Dylan and a happy stockbroker. It's a
long way down from the 68th floor and take-out
foods don't keep too well in ticker-tape parades.

Lenox Hill Hospital takes credit cards and the
tall ships make me cry.
I get propositioned
coming out of Sardi's
so I hold my fur coat
closer under my chin and
hail a cab.

"*Chelsea Hotel,*" I say, checking into the
room Dylan Thomas may or may not have
passed out in after a long night boozing
at the White Horse Tavern.
I discover, instead,
the blood of Sid Vicious' girlfriend,
and am desperately in need of a dry
Martini before trying to scrub the stains.

Thanksgiving sneaks up on me when I least expect it.
I turn on the Macy's Parade, eat canned spaghetti and
wonder about the meaning of time
in a bottle.

Winters come and go,
so do I. The lights stay on
in Times Square and Central Park has a
rape crisis center next to the merry-go-round.

I unfasten my seat belt and say hello to a beautiful lady.

SMILE

SoHo is another story. Phyllis has her gallery
and Red hasn't yet drunk the Liquid-Plumr. I
give up a home, a complete collection of Fiestaware
and my major appliances to live in the middle
of a reconverted artificial flower factory
in midtown Manhattan.

The things we do when we don't know 30.

I sell my piano to my dentist. Bridgework
will now be Brooklyn, George Washington
and a tunnel called Lincoln.

I eat donuts sitting on a stool
next to the methadone clinic
watching men push heavy racks of clothing up
Eighth Avenue. The boxed fruits and
vegetables drone on in colors of red, gold,
purple and green. Steaming coffee rises
around me like fog over Haleakalā Crater.

I fit in here.

Just like I fit in at IBM
the oval office
Edwards Air Force Base
my mother's kitchen
Times Square
a young boy's bed
a campsite in Barcelona
an all-night wedding chapel in Reno
the Waldorf

a graveyard in Erie, PA.

I hunt Bengal tigers in China and then have time
for a quick trip to the moon on
Buddha's rockets. I volunteer in a
mental hospital, then become
the patient. I've been living
for nearly 2,000 years and I see
Apple computers becoming
Jeff Koons and
the Russian Revolution.

It's a series of snapshots,
life.

Smile.

This picture of life. Take the moment
for the moment. The lights are strong,
a life in focus.

Smile.

You're in frame
we're in frame
we look back
we dream
we ache with wants.

Smile.

> *We try to fit in.*

BACK TO PARADISE

when last seen here i was
slithering down a lamppost
buckling under my own knees
i was so far removed from life
and yet i remember the cracks in the sidewalks
the bloodstained aprons in balducci's
drinking pina coladas on waverly place
and then fucking bill after waiting ten
years for his body and his mouth

a presence
that had now become nothing more than a
magnet for heroin

no pain, mama, we felt nothing
but swimming kisses and dying hugs
driving around i sit on top of the inside door
handle of his cab so the meter won't run

i wait by the curb on houston street, a shooting
gallery takes him in to score and fly us

        back to paradise

a day tripper booking passage for weeks
maybe months
a clock is something best left to movado
and smart phones

i work on a different principle and study the
view from a five-story walk-up
flat on my back

hear the bells ring
in washington square park
feed the pigeons anchovy pizza
and give a bum a quarter

we were dogs in heat bill and i
and when we finally managed to pull ourselves
apart from that hot bony mess
the white emptiness of our love
the breath of fire consumed us

i schedule meetings with literary agents
and stork club dinners

        yes it was new york

and there were things to do
from every window
my glass pane existence
a matter of movement and cash flow

when last seen here
i was making appointments
with death
bowing out before the final curtain
not willing to become a bottom line obit in the
new york times

when last seen here
bill got on a plane for san francisco
headed south to santa cruz and began
picking apples to keep his mind off his body

it is july 4th and I come back to this mad island
to salute lady liberty
because we are one and
being free is everything.

ANOTHER YANKEE IN ARS LONGA

Broadway melody hums along neon moons
glowing with street walkers
pimps and hassidic jews
the only city in the western world
to speak shalom in 52 languages
kisses sailors by day
beggars by night

Ziggurats dance tall on 38th street
and shout *good morning mr. armani*
pushing coat racks past the
methadone clinic
watching the children play hopscotch
the sky is mottled with energy
and taxis line up in pairs

It's great to be alive to be
walking these streets
a chorus girl
a lawyer
a secretary
a dog trainer
a mistress of mercy
chewing her belgian waffle
at lutèce
drinking mimosas
with an ex-governor
making deposits in her merrill lynch account

The city speaks for everyone
the city whispers

in sign language
and breathes like a baby

When all else fails
she goes mute, blacks out
and asks for a hand
while radio city music hall
bleats out the maple leaf rag and
we skate over rockefeller's
ice, brothers
in arms
sisters
in legs

The bodies beautiful kicking their alls
kick up dreams
kick downtown
kicking away death
until no more kicks are left

Just a bloodless cry and a cigar stand
selling nitrous oxide bullets
a line forms
a line dissipates
this city welcomes us
this city needs us

We are this city
wayward pilgrims toasting the waves
our past in double-breasted pea coats

signing declarations
in turkey blood

> *e pluribus unim*
> *coitis interruptus*
> *of thee I sing*

Madonna, another yankee in ars longa
warbles while boston sleeps
and bakes beans
this crawling city peddles her future
in pushcarts
and tells us
that everything
is all right here
quite all right

Isn't It Rich?

IV.

SUNDAY IN THE POOL WITH FRED

Sunday in the pool with Fred
won't win a Pulitzer
any Tony Awards
or the New York Drama Desk prize
but it certainly beats sitting in a
lonely, air-conditioned apartment
on Doheny Drive.

Fred and I have been pool friends for years.
Was a time when I thought we might even
get married and have kids.

He's handsome
successful
witty
jewish
and
gay.

That would have been okay with me.

He loves kids and I wasn't
Ms. Monogamous
myself.
We could have had
the best of both worlds
because this was before AIDS
before herpes
and before he settled down with another man
not unlike himself.

I'm floating in the newly-plastered pool
floating back to the early days
the very early days.
We even met in a jacuzzi in Palm Springs
and our relationship erupted like those
whirling jets.

But the night I always remember is the
night we had sex.

It was his birthday.

We'd been to Chasen's for dinner
and ate chili sitting at the best table
with a view of Peggy Lee and the heart surgeon
Christian Barnard.
Our fevers were rising and my major artery
was pumping hard with want.

We drank a lot of Mumm's,

then went back
to his place to continue the fantasy.
Heavy petting led me to the bathroom
to retrieve a false eyelash;
him to the bedroom for the encounter.

There was a lot of in and out in
Beverly Hills that night but
morning had to come and reality
set in the way it does after too much
champagne
cocaine

and not enough
foreplay.

We never had sex again but we still
spend nights together.
The adjoining hotel rooms in places like
San Francisco
Fire Island and Martha's Vineyard remind us
of what could have been.

> We don't ever talk about

that birthday
that evening
those dreams.
At least I don't.

I just come and spend Sunday in the pool
with Fred because I know it's the
California thing to do.

MOTHER LOVE

I dream about being a mother,
instead I take a lover of 19.

He surfs and speaks in double negatives.
I take him to his rugby practice and
photograph his youngness.

I hold him like a baby after we fuck
then I pack his lunch and watch him
ride off in the white dawn of innocence
on a 10-speed bike.

I cook his favorite dinner
baked potato and steak sandwich,
plump and pink.

I wait by the window, watching
the sun go under the ocean.
The steak is cold and tough when the
moon rises. I freeze the chocolate cheesecake
         along with my diaphragm
and eat canned mushroom soup
all summer long.

Five hundred and forty moonrises later
Roger returns.
He drives a Datsun now

and is old enough to drink.
His grammar is good
but his knowledge of tenses still needs work.

He is all tongue and muscle;
I am just a little older.
I turn off the gas
and hope the broccoli soufflé won't fall.

He makes me come too soon
again and again.
>   *The night is everything.*

THE LIFE OF A SHRIMP

The jumbo shrimp, gleamy pink in their
shells, are invited to all the best parties
in town. They ride in cool comfort, beds
of ice to keep them moist and chill.
In carpeted Cadillacs,
they weave through the canyons and
hills of Beverly.

They lie down next to
champagne and
rise to occasions filled with
frozen swans and bouquets of
coral gladioli.

A focal point, these prawns are dipped in
scarlet sauces,
steamy mustards,
tartar'ed dills and
sometimes sucked raw
by movie stars, press agents and a
hungry actor along for the ride.

With fanfares they beckon, butterflied,
splayed, wide-eyed and
deveined, these royal crustaceans
command attention, if only for an
evening, a moment,
an eyeblink.

I make my way to the banquet table,
blinded by the bride's white of the
silk. The crystal and sterling silver

backdrop frame these mounds of plump
firm delicacies.

I spot my prey. I stab it with
the flick of my wrist and
raise it to my lips and
one swift gulp tells me
that heaven exists here on
Coldwater Canyon Drive and
the life of yet another shrimp has just
become oral history.

LIFESTYLES OF THE POOR AND UNKNOWN

He's a day laborer reclining poolside
on Labor Day in a
pool of blood,
struck down by a falling DC-9
en route from Guadalajara to LAX.

He's a black teenage boy driving a
Jaguar in Malibu, valet parking at Geoffrey's
so he'll be able to score his next fix, scope
out his next heist, make his next stop, a
JD home
and we're not talking
Juris Prudence
here.

She's a young pregnant runaway drinking Tequila and
Tecate, walking Hollywood Boulevard in search of
a star. She lands on James Dean, has deformed
twins and goes on national TV pleading for a
kidney.

She's a Fresno librarian by day, searching for
dried nuts by night (after all, this is the raisin
capital of the world), only to encounter a madman
rapist needing another notch in his seven-grained
belt.

They're the perfect working couple, Ma and Pa
doctor, treating the sexual dysfunctionals all
week long, only to prescribe Percodan, Dilaudid and

crystal methamphetamine for themselves during Saturday
cocktail hours and Sunday brunches.

Lip-smackers hit suburbia and life imitates itself.

He's a preteen schoolboy with AIDS who isn't
allowed to learn Spanish, he isn't allowed to know
that Columbus discovered America by dint of a wrong
turn and he won't be rat racing to the American dream:

> How to make chocolate chip cookies for
> fun and profit.

Stakes are high for the rich and famous,
and why not: they've got fatter contracts,
more residuals and better
press coverage
than our poor and unknown.

When Lady Liberty first said, "Give me your poor, your
hungry, your tired huddled masses,"
she wasn't asking
for Miley Cyrus, a real housewife of Orange County or
Caitlyn Jenner,
no ma'am.

She wanted a lace tatter from Sweden,
a Russian dressmaker in a Stalinesque vein,
a Polish butcher,
a baker,
a candelabra maker so Michael Douglas
could play Caesars Palace

She wanted you and me, babe.

So we came, we headed west and sprawled out like
bicycle spokes and a lot of us
got conquered
by our own greed,
our own lust,
our own misfortune and
our own destiny,
but we carried on with the hard business of
living. We carried on as best we knew how.

We kept our lights burning until the end,

because we are the poor and unknown and
only through this poem can our lifestyles be told
and only through this poem will you know us,
and only then might you care.

Isn't It Rich?

V.

THE GENETICS OF DINING

Brad speaks to his princess,
who has momentarily stepped into the powder room
to re-establish her presence as
queen of the night.

Ducking paparazzi, she clings to the bronze
banister of success
and succeeds
in escaping notoriety
by the mere act of
vomiting neatly.

> *"Too many calamari,"* she exclaims,
> *"not enough clams."*

It is precisely this point about which
she has fought with Brad and a coterie of waiters,
including the wine steward with his fermenting corks,
El Capitan, also known as Dimitri,
and the dessert boy
who awaits his turn to flambé the bananas.

The art of fine dining cannot be acquired, for it is
a genetic trait, and very recessive,
being passed from mother to son via a continental lover or two,
while paternally it will skip a generation until

Voila: A Stomach Is Born.

Amazing we ever get any enjoyment
out of one of
life's most necessary pastimes.

But enjoy we do,

eat we do,

America,

incessant,

excessive,

bulimic and

coddled,

this princess reigns supreme,

while the rest of the world appears to be

genetically imbalanced and hungry,

hungry for more.

A SWEET TOOTH FILLS THE AIR

alaskan   fireworks   freeze   the   ass   off

an eagle when they

      fly

              off

                          handles

bruisey, violet-veined birthmark

on my
knees

         i beg

     you

head tilted back

accepting your haircut   into my mouth

a sweet tooth fills the air

AS LONG TWILIGHT CALLS

In the cabin on Cold Creek Trail
stinging clean air
runs through my veins here.

I love this country
I love these woods. High greens, velvet
they talk to me.

The sun plays with
the last leaves of the day
as long twilight calls.

I want to build a fire but
I failed Bluebirds and can't bear
a recurring nightmare. Aw hell,
why not lug a log in,
light it up and order a pizza
to share with myself. Settling in
I write this purple-prosed poem:

> *The moonlight urges me on. Listen to*
> *the night crackle with cool warmth.* *

*It's really too hot for a fire in July, so
I just curl up with some soft-core pornography
instead.

Isn't It Rich?

VI.

A FAR CRY FROM GITCHE GUMEE

I thought you had to have blonde hair to
live in California
blonde hair, blue eyes, low on brains.

> *Never figured I'd be in the running here.*

Running a mouse race in Reeboks
treading the mills
flexing the quads
squeezing the butt.

> *Aw shit, man, like wow*
> *fer sure, fer sure.*

Why don't you learn how to speak
without chewing Juicy Fruit
your tongue is not what's at issue
here lady
and your BMW is far from a
glass coach.

You're the cowbell of the ball
your big foot
in your mouth more than
your slipper.

Stride along
glide along
the red, red carpet, shagged and dragged
behind you, from under you
disguising the stains of your past
with very plastic surgery

skillfully executed by the masked man
once known as your husband.

Am I getting through missy
or is the ether still flying through your cortex
your gray matter
doesn't matter much to me.

White heron from the east
wearing sunblock balancing on a
gossamer leg
flirting with flies
on the shore a dull deep marsh for my bed,

    a far cry from Gitche Gumee

but ready for love

    CAW CAW

Ready when you are
pale-haired maiden comes
down from the clouds

    Who's gonna love ya now, baby?

she says to me, I say to her
we look around at the emptiness
of the city, the spread-fingered freeways
choke our desire
the stars on Hollywood Boulevard

are spit-shined by a
honeymooning couple from Kokomo,
Wisconsin and a
migrant worker on his
way to Needles
sells maps to Rock Hudson's home.

We fall into the tar pits
and muck around with
some dead athletes for a while
freebasing can be fatal we hear,
lucky to resurface at Georgette Klinger's
aesthetician to the stars,
mud packs intact.

A hair, an eye, a body
are finely tuned
by these resident aliens
who happen to be a little
just a little
like me we decide.

O, beauty is painful when it's really working
        so much to do
        too much to remember
        so high a price

You hear me, huh?
Do you?

Hear
me?

THIS POEM LAUGHS

The poem I want to write
reeks of old good loves
Mediterranean cruises
and Garbo in *Camille*.

But the poem that speaks to me
won't take part in 8 x 10 glossies
won't cater to dancing around
my sun-bleached living room
floating above the ocean
with a man I love.

This poem laughs
hysterical
wild
laughs at me
in my fantasy
wants a baby
to fuse the vision
knows the beautiful man
moves instead from
flower to flower
stops only at random, if at all,
if ever,
then flies into the surf
free.
         Alone.

I follow the path
with my eyes

strong eyes
a familiar awareness.
It's the heart
that stops cold. The heart won't take
it anymore. Can't
pump the data.

Stops
dead.
The heart, my heart
turns a quiet beat into a dull ache.

This poem, meanwhile, this word keeper
pledged to secrecy
keeps everything hidden away
tucked in for the winter
and just waits.

It just waits for that
certain precious moment,
another wave-wrecked spring.

Maybe that, yes.

MA

Ma is working on husband number four.

"This is it," she says, dreaming of
paisley printed boxer shorts and
a new Saks charge card.

"And he's young, too."

The phone conversation
between California and Florida
heats up like two teenagers yakking away,
lots of words, no substance.

Ma finds out his youth is 72 years and
climbing.

Christ, she's had it with Mt. Olympus and
wheelchairs rolling down freeway off-ramps
like over-tired truckers
and early bird dinners of clams and canned peas.

> *What muscle there is when money is
> involved.*

Ma buries number two in Philadelphia
liberty cracking all the way to the bank
and sits mourning over Miami,
her vices keep her company.

The Kool Lites,
vodka and red Seconals
help pass the time, moons

she counts
outside her bedroom window
until she alone can collect
Social
Security.

Number three makes a brief appearance at the altar.
A divorced Jewish
dentist posing as a man.

"In sickness and in health, till veils do us part,"
he recites, stumbling over the *I do's* that quickly pale.

Broom handles, vibrators and young boys bring the
curtain down on Act III.

Ma assembles tuna sandwiches for ten dollar tips
at the bridge club
dyes her hair blonde.

*"Marilyn Monroe doesn't hold all the cards
on suffering,"* she tells me,
proud to share her birthday with the Queen of Pain.

Ma's head hurts,
her back aches,
her fingers cramp from
the mohair cardigans
she cable knits
for Cleveland exiles,
divorcees skin diving
in Bimini.

"The pirates are still out there," I tell her,
listening to the click-clack
of her needles over the wires,
subway trains bound for nowhere.

Ma,
a wool puller nonpareil...
I miss her more
than she'll ever know.

Isn't It Rich?

VII.

ORDER IN THE AIR

Skipping through my mind bank
I find a collection of old loves. I
blow off the dust and wipe sweat
from my brow, staring into the face
of another heartbreak. I smile,
I cry, I remember
the kisses in the wind and the daughter
wanting to be born.

The koto strings are thick and
my Japanese is bad. I hand the cab driver
a scrap of paper and he shakes his head. My
apartment is cold, crowded,
squeezed between bolts of green and pink neon.
Somehow the steaming water pulls me into an
ancient world of ceremony.

And tea.

I sink into a tall wooden tub and remember
my black hair wrapped around ivory combs,
my obi closing in on me like a warm
cocoon and a quiet voice follows me down
the path.

Snow fell like feathers
and rain warmed my cheeks.

There was order in the air.

I pulse with love and the tiny footsteps bound
in silk are my own.

THE CLOT THICKENS

Chianti Classico bottles are dripping in wax,
magenta, fuchsia and winter white they glow
in the dark even while the wine is being drunk
gulped and slugged
sec et brut
blanc et rouge.

Her cheeks are ruby-esque too,
blushing pink, like pearls thrown before the swine
a man unwittingly imitates.

Mimicry without malice, he thinks he apes
without intent, yet the *oinks* come
oh yes, the oinks of sure love burst forth
once too loudly, way too often.

These are the squeals of a conglomerate past
he refuses to acknowledge as his heritage.

Man, a word three letters shy of
maniac,
he adores the hunt,
a conquering Cassanova who ogles,
leers, conjures, finally fabricates a
plot tailor-made for canopied beds
to capture his
objet desire

  A wanted woman.

She, unsuspecting, quiet, open-hearted
she yields like gravy
dripping, creamy and oh, so spreadable.

It is the bedroom, a site where Margaret
Mead's bones spring forth archaeologically
speaking through the monogrammed sheets of
time, silken and woven with destiny to
soak up the fresh blood of a
young girl's dream.

The clot thickens:

*Her reverie of a future filled with hopeless perfection
teems with history.*

It is the bedroom where a family,
an equal opportunity employer and
an unswerving adoration
are all born
again and again
over and over
the scene plays throughout the ages
to an audience of actors.

Beds aside, it's standing room only and rain checks
are redeemable.

8:00 PM and the curtain is about to rise;
the Chianti Classico bottles are dripping in wax,
their silent flickerings in tune with a hushed
crowd that stares fixedly at the stage and
begins to mouth the lines in anticipation
of the unknown,

> *hoping that this time might be different.*

BEAN CAKES AND YOU

Every pebble is in a place

ordered by God and Zen monks.

They breathe quietly and watch my mind

churning around like butter.

The air smells of lavender and musk. Will I

ever get enough? Christmas is coming to

New York, but here,

in Nara, I think only of

bean cakes

and you.

Isn't It Rich?

VIII.

SCREWTOPIA

I can't push myself on a man
get hard and try to pound it into him.
I can only watch when some man does this
to me. I watch him as he tries to
undress me. Untie my Reeboks. Pull off
my panties.

Drag me to the bedroom.

I watch with anger and hurt as I
realize this is no contest
I'm losing anyway
and I feel my neck snap
as he yanks my hair back
to another night when making love
was good and I came with the moon
on the ocean because we knew each
other's bodies like we knew
how to walk.

Who is this bearded lawyer
taking me into his hands instead of
a statute, this Porsche driver
I drink Dom Pérignon with
because it tastes good
and why won't he let me go home
to sleep, why do I
lie in his big messy bed listening
to him snore and count tax shelters
while the phone rings with more
troubled people
crying into the night?

Who is this bastard thrusting his
tongue and fingers into my mouth,
trying to swallow me like a lotus
blossom only to realize I died
three months ago with the winter?

He thinks he's a landowner, my body
his territory, holding the deed from
dinner, drinks, a movie and American
Express. He's got rights, he's got
degrees.

He's got balls.

But I don't like them and
I think I'm
going to puke.

I remember my psychiatrist looking at
me with his sad wise eyes, his cigar
ash getting ready to fall as he somberly states:

> "Where does it say in the Torah
> that thou shalt suck cock?"

The gagging subsides as dawn lets me
find my clothes and I grab my chance
to slink away,
a lone crab on the shore.

SOMETHING FISHY

I stand in front of the fish counter at
the Ralph's Market and think about
my first abortion.

After sixteen years of infertility, no one is more stunned
than I.

Actually, I refuse to acknowledge the pregnancy and
only as I lay on the cold table,
bare feet up in even colder stirrups, do I
begin to cry for a baby
I will never see.

The salmon look very firm and pink, but
it is the octopus that I choose.
I like tentacles, I like hooks.

It was my psychiatrist who urged me
to be more open to the possibility
of men
again.

I don't blame him for what happens,
and in fact
find myself pregnant again
six months
later.

A family reunion in Las Vegas is the backdrop
for the seduction. My siblings and I have just
seen Joan Rivers' midnight show before I help
a twenty-one year old
come
of age
at the Tropicana Hotel.

Quarters are strewn all over the bed;
he has just won
a giant jackpot,
o, the irony,
I think, struggling to take off my tuxedo.

His name is Gary and I need
his blondeness
around me. Does he think my tiny cries
are those of satisfaction
or does he know
my desperation?

These cries echo into the Vegas night,
unheard, as roulette wheels come creaking
to empty finishes and
the sounds of cards
mingle with early-morning wanderers
unable to remember their dreams.

I am living my dream, holding it, breathing it
and
fucking it.

They say the days in Las Vegas go on all night
and that the nights are so black you
can sleep with your eyes open.
But there is no sleep.

I am wheeled out of UCI Med Center
and bleed for weeks.

My psychiatrist has little to say;
he is getting ready for his yearly sabbatical
to the mountains of Mendocino.

It is Christmas and I give my tuxedo to the
Salvation Army. I look at the ocean
outside my living room window and
I see thousands of perfect hands
opening their
translucent fingers,
calling me back to the water...
the cold, dark grey water.

I walk away from the fish counter and take my
place
at the end of a long
slow line.

Isn't It Rich?

IX.

NEO-HAIKUS AND THINGS

it was leap year
we'd known each other for ten minutes
before leaping into bed.

        my lips are siamese
        kittens purring
        in the wind

              old men walk
              on gold
              when the end comes

i couldn't remember love ever
being like this
maybe because it never was

        pale moon floats
        on a curly lake
        needing so much love

god likes me to
breathe sunshine
once in a while

NOT THE RITZ

I am not a rock, I am a mountain
who has died once
in a downtown Los Angeles hospital
on the eighteenth floor
surrounded by nuns and Mexicans
a team of Jewish doctors and
hundreds of feet of tubing

I float for five days
high over the world and when
I finally decide to come back
my first words are:

"Where's my purse?"

They get my heart going again
but only I know
how empty it is
only I know a part of it will never
breathe again

It is Thanksgiving and I
leave one hospital for another
high on a cliff
overlooking the ocean where gulls
cry and bird-of-paradise
grow in great clumps outside
my barred window.

My friend Natalie Wood has drowned and
I feel nothing.

I meet my doctor that afternoon,
he is handsome with a full graying beard,
his pants are too short and he
wears brown leather Topsider shoes.

> *"This isn't the Ritz, you know,"* he says
> *"and you're really fucked."*

It is hard to swallow but I eat
turkey soup and green jello. My
room has a closet, some dresser drawers and
a single bed where, I'd been told,
Joan Kennedy once slept.

There are no faucets on the bathtub and no
locks on my door.

That's okay, I'm not interested in bathing,
I only want to sleep
and sleep.

But every hour, when they come with
their flashlights, shining their arcs of light
on my face,
my eyes are still open
wide open.

This goes on far too long.

THE DANCE CRITIC

I met him at a party. I was a
dance critic. He was a
dancer. A ballerino,
a primo assoluto, with an emphasis
on the ass.

"*I'm dancing* The Nutcracker *next week,*"
he said,
revealing a ravishingly sexy,
chipped front tooth
that I would later learn
had come from his
having cracked it
on a urinal.

"*Are you the Prince?*" I asked,
"*because if you're the Prince...*"
my voice trailed off, thoughts of rabid sugar plum
fairies dancing in my head,
while the review
I fashioned in my mind
was already stellar,
because, of course,
he could be nothing less than the Prince who would
carry me off on his charger,
his steed,
his studliness.

"*Yeah. The Prince. That's me.*"
He nodded, a full, thick head of jet black hair
framing his face like a B-list Bruegel.
This was said, devoid of irony,

because this Prince operated in an
irony-free zone.
But I was already hooked
on this nobleman called James,
who was also a two-time
world-champion
kickboxer in the
Filipino art form
known as Sikaran Arnis,
which accounted for his
scabby knuckles,
his terpsichorean turnout,
however,
still a turn-on
for *moi*
especially since
he was eighteen years
younger.

For me,
the performance began
after he'd shed his
red *Nutcracker* cavalier costume,
one that had come
from the Bolshoi,
the red, a neo-Communist thing,
scarlet right down to his
flaming ballet slippers,
when he was fucking me
so hard
so deep
so long
I thought I was going to get

fucked to death.

No such luck.

But the dance critic was, finally...
at the dance.
When we were together
he was my Nureyev.
I was his Fonteyn,
fucking to Prokofiev's
Romeo and Juliet,
a dance that for me,
could have bourrée'd us
into eternity.

Of course, what this Prince really wanted was
an action movie career,
because his
legs, he said, were becoming *plie-challenged,*
his *jetés* no longer buoyant and his
pirouettes had petered out.

I felt for him, surely,
but since he entered my life,
which he did,
lock, stock and dance belt,
moving in to take care of me,
because I'd gotten sciatica from
well,
too much fucking,
I told him,

If I can walk, dear James,
yes, oh, yes, you can act,

to which he responded by
fucking me
again
and
        again.

But even I knew
that this wild *pas de deux*
would, no doubt, have the shelf life
of a quail's egg,
with the *coup de grâce* coming,
not when I discovered
that this Prince of mine had OCD,
nor that he
suffered from
borderline personality disorder,
no, none of that stuff,

        but that
        he, *arrrghhh*, voted
        for Bush,
        ferfuckingchrissake.

No, this great love would not end up
like the *Nutcracker*,
where I could have my Prince and
bed him too,
but would prove
far worse than
sciatica for my health.

Then again, this was my pattern:

        falling for losers, but still filled with hope.

THIS VERY MOMENT

Can't be happier than at this moment watching
Bogart crack the *Maltese Falcon*
can't be happier smoking a Thai stick
snorting some smack
sailing the Virgins
canalling Amsterdam
snorkeling the Canaries
fucking a surfer
eating sushi
skiing Squaw
zenning in Kyoto
limo-ing the South of France
parasailing Acapulco
facial-ing in Baden-Baden
strumming for a Lord *(well, maybe that one we could do without)*

sunsetting in Laguna
wining in Pommard
cable car-ing Hyde Street
rose gathering in the Tuileries
penning a poem.

Well, maybe just a small one
yes, a small poem might make
me happier than I am,
even now,
at this very moment.

The text of *Isn't It Rich? A Novella in Verse* is set in ITC Giovanni, the work of California type designer Robert Slimbach in 1986. His goal was to create a thoroughly contemporary font with classic old style proportions. He succeeded.

The chapter headings are set in the forever classic and clean Futura, a design by German Paul Renner in 1927. Contrary to the easy assumption, Renner was not a part of the Bauhaus Movement but he shared the ideology.

This book is designed by Gordy Grundy.

Single Cuts Nº. 1 (2014)
5" x 7"

KATRIEN DE BLAUWER
Cover Artist

    Katrien De Blauwer calls herself a "photographer without a camera." The Belgian artist collects and recycles photos and pictures from old magazines to create stunning collages of distant mood and place. These fragmentary images evoke faded memories that are quickly brought to the fore. In turn, the viewer becomes a character in De Blauwer's stories.

    De Blauwer shows extensively throughout Europe. Her work has been featured in numerous publications and appears often in the *New York Times*.

    The work of Katrien De Blauwer can be found at www.KatrienDeBlauwer.com

Charles Bukowski

MARK HANAUER
Photographer

Photographer Mark Hanauer moves seamlessly between genres, whether it be evocative portraits, ethereal meditations, or visceral landscapes. He combines experience with a searching eye, staying within the moment, while exploring the technical, visual and emotional possibilities of his surroundings. With portraiture, he engages his subjects so that he or she is a collaborator and not merely an object. Hanauer says, "I prefer to find fresh, creative solutions, working to satisfy my subject's needs, and to find and capture their inner truth."

The work of the Santa Monica based artist has appeared in GQ, Forbes, Time, Esquire, Rolling Stone and many other magazines and national advertising campaigns.

His artistic efforts can be found at www.MarkHanauer.com.

Photo by Mark Hanauer

VICTORIA LOOSELEAF
Author

Victoria Looseleaf lives and loves in Los Angeles. As an award-winning dance and arts writer, the redhead provocateur has been filing datelines from her many lives in Abu Dhabi, Vienna, Havana, Monte Carlo, Tel Aviv, Berlin, Amsterdam, Zürich, Buenos Aires, Athens, Lyon and dozens more points on the compass.

Once a professional harpist, her albums *Harpnosis* and *Beyond Harpnosis* can be found on the turntables of discerning listeners everywhere.

The Looseleaf Report, a late night staple of Los Angeles and New York television, offered celebrity interviews, humor and underground arts insights with over 400 broadcast shows.

Today, Looseleaf is steadfast as one of journalism's few remaining freelance writers.

Isn't It Rich? is Victoria Looseleaf's first book of poetry.

GORDY GRUNDY
PUBLISHERS
www.GordyGrundy.com

www.ingramcontent.com/pod-product-compliance
Lightning Source LLC
Chambersburg PA
CBHW022113090426
42743CB00008B/837